Curriculum Visions

Exploring
evolution

World history

4.5 billion	3.5 billion	2.5 billion	2.1 billion	600 million	450 million	420 million

Fiirst living things with more than one cell.

Plants and 'insects' (arthropods) leave the sea and colonise the land.

Origin of the Earth.

First living things are microbes and live in oceans.

Earth's atmosphere starts to include oxygen.

A great explosion of life including the first animals with skeletons. This time is called the Cambrian. Fish, shelled animals and many more all date from this time. Famous for trilobites.

First animal survive entire with oxygen fr the air

360 million: first ferns on land, early ammonites, sharks and crabs in the sea.

Another great collision in space, and dinosaurs become extinct. Mammals begin to dominate the world.

350 million	250 million	225 million	155 million	65 million	6 million	2 million

Carboniferous large conifer trees (source of most of the world's coal). First reptiles.

Most living things become extinct perhaps because of a collision with a rocky body from space.

Earliest dinosaurs.

First birds evolve.

First man-like animals evolve.

First modern man. The Stone Age begins.

One of the famous Galapagos' (Darwin's) finches.

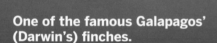

Contents

Look up the **bold** words in the glossary on page 32 of this book.

The early Earth

What happened to our world in the past? What was it like compared to today? That is a very big question.

Our world has changed time after time since it formed from a mass of dust about four and a half billion years ago. At the very start it was completely **molten**, a huge glowing globe spinning through space. Then, over millions and millions of years, it cooled on the surface, and what had been liquid solidified into rock. The Earth's crust had been made.

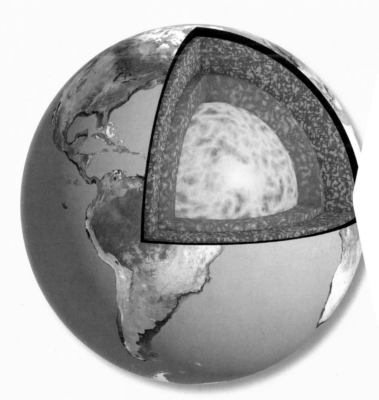

The pictures show the Earth gathering together from rocks and dust (left), then how it first became a molten planet (centre), before getting a crust (right). The cut-out shows that the Earth is made of many layers. The innermost one is still molten.

 How did the Earth start?

The first life

The cooling of the Earth is still going on. But billions of years later the crust is only a few tens of kilometres thick. That is because rock is such a good **insulator**. Under the crust, the rock is still very hot. It is the source of volcanoes.

Volcanoes are the source of so much that we find on the surface. Everything we know – rock, soil, water and air – comes from volcanoes. When volcanoes erupt they may cause disasters to modern life, but without them there would be no life at all.

The first life may have started around hot springs. We find traces of life in the oceans from about three and a half billion years ago.

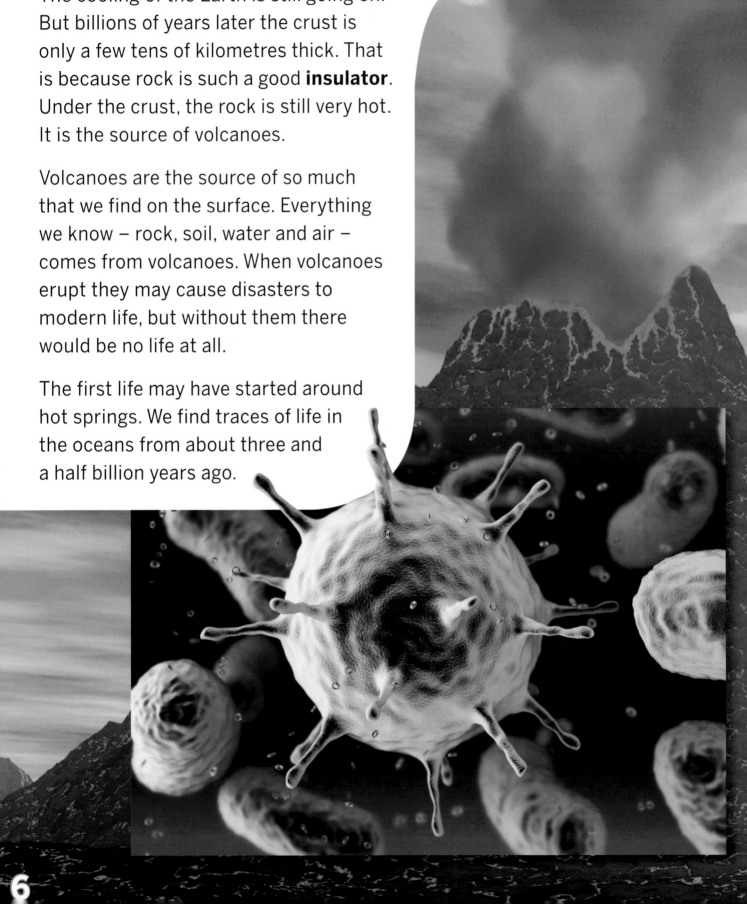

- The early Earth did not have much of an **atmosphere**, and what there was had very little oxygen in it. So life could not survive on land. That is why the first living things began in water – especially in oceans.
- The water for the oceans came from the water vapour released by volcanoes.
- Most of the early life was soft-bodied, and has left little trace.

Q **Where did the first life live, and what was it?**

The earliest kinds of living thing that we know about are in the oceans. They are **microbes**. Three and a half billion years ago they began to form in large numbers, making sticky 'glues' that trapped grains of sand into knobbly 'rocks'. They are still doing it today. Here they are in Australia. (They are called stromatolites).

Common ancestor

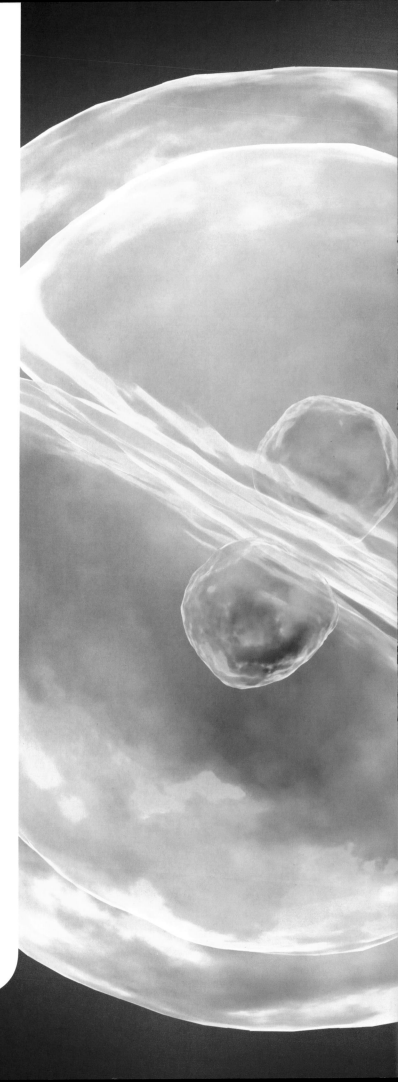

You may not think we have much in common with the first tiny microbe that ever lived, 3.8 billion years ago. But we do. Something like that microbe is the common ancestor of all things alive today.

The famous scientist, Charles Darwin, recognised this in the 19th century. Today, we know far more about how life works than Darwin was able to, and so we know that all life is made of **cells** which split up to make copies of themselves (like the cell in this picture). Inside each cell is a liquid, and floating about inside it is a little parcel of information which tells the cell how to make new copies. It is known as DNA.

Just twenty simple chemicals (amino acids) were needed to make our common ancestor, and that is still true even though life is enormously varied today.

Special particles (proteins) inside the cell work to change food into energy and make everything else in the cell.

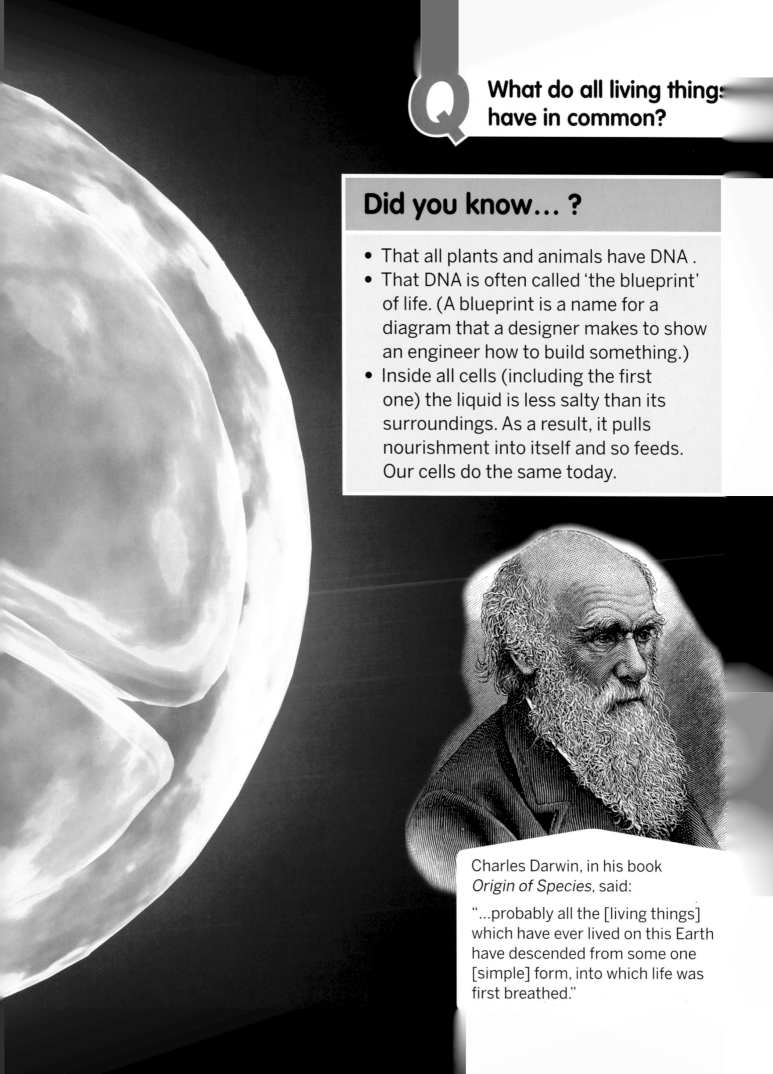

Q What do all living things have in common?

Did you know… ?

- That all plants and animals have DNA .
- That DNA is often called 'the blueprint' of life. (A blueprint is a name for a diagram that a designer makes to show an engineer how to build something.)
- Inside all cells (including the first one) the liquid is less salty than its surroundings. As a result, it pulls nourishment into itself and so feeds. Our cells do the same today.

Charles Darwin, in his book *Origin of Species*, said:

"...probably all the [living things] which have ever lived on this Earth have descended from some one [simple] form, into which life was first breathed."

Skeletons

The first living things did not have skeletons. They were soft-bodied. There are still many soft-bodied things around today, such as most plants and many animals like slugs.

But skeletons have many uses. The first animals to get a skeleton used it as a kind of shell. This protected their bodies and also helped to hold them up – and as a result they could be bigger. The dinosaurs could not have become gigantic if they had not developed strong skeletons. We could not stand up without skeletons.

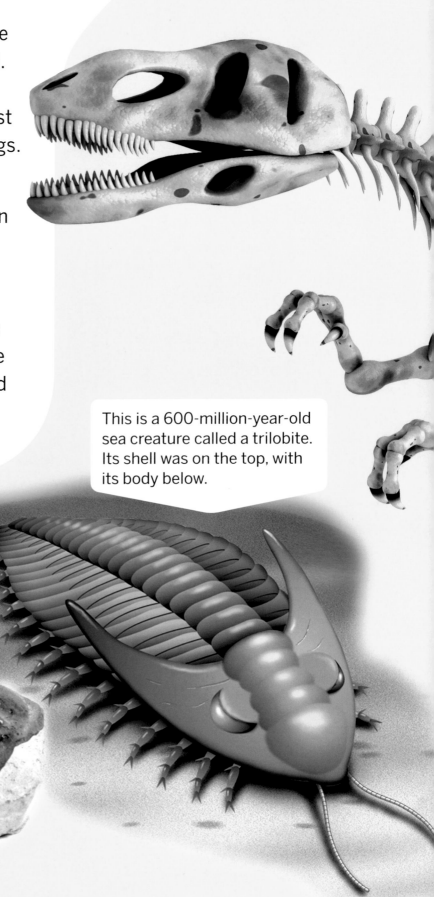

This is a 600-million-year-old sea creature called a trilobite. Its shell was on the top, with its body below.

A plaster cast (solid) made of a trilobite shell from a hollow shape (mould) in a rock. It was then coloured.

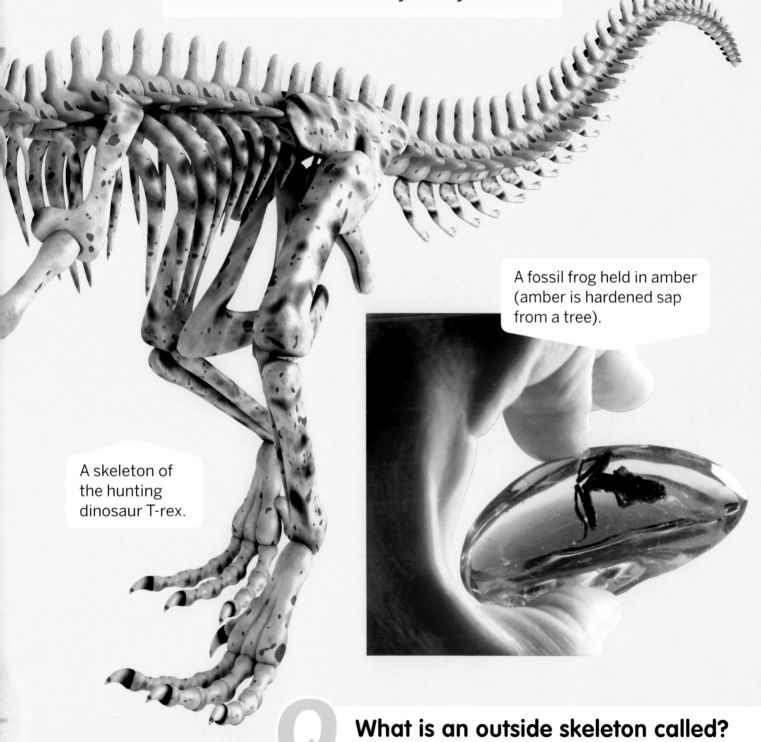

Did you know… ?

- An outside skeleton – a shell – makes it impossible to grow beyond a certain size.
- Many skeletons are solid and heavy – but bird bones are hollow and lightweight, which is one reason they can fly.

A fossil frog held in amber (amber is hardened sap from a tree).

A skeleton of the hunting dinosaur T-rex.

Q What is an outside skeleton called?

How fossils form

We know about the evolution of life on Earth through the fossils that have formed.

This diagram shows the way it sometimes works. This is a coastal lagoon. Plants grow in the shallow water, and many animals live in the water and above it.

New silt and sand is always settling out on the bottom. When a plant or animal dies, it sinks to the bottom. There it usually starts to rot and other animals feed on its flesh. Soon only the skeleton remains to be buried.

Just occasionally, a dead animal is buried by silt, mud and sand before it is eaten. Then the whole animal is preserved. As it is buried under more sand, silt and mud, the layers turn to rock.

Millions of years later the rocks may be worn away, and then the fossils appear in cliffs or river banks.

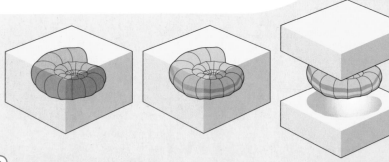

A cast is a solid made from minerals that have replaced the animal. A mould is a hollow space showing where the animal once was.

Fossils are animals and plants buried in mud, silt or sand. This protects them. But, over time, the soft parts dissolve away and new liquids replace them. These liquids slowly harden, so that eventually what was once the remains of a plant or an animal becomes solid stone. This is a piece of fossil tree, but it is no longer made of wood; it is now stone.

Did you know… ?

- Most fossils are found in rocks that were laid down under the sea because the sea bed does not have strong currents, and so the dead animal is not moved about and broken up as it would be in a river.
- Fossils forming in mud rocks (shales) show more detail than those in sandstone.
- You never find fossils in rocks like granite because they were formed from molten lava.

Q **What is a fossil cast and what is a mould?**

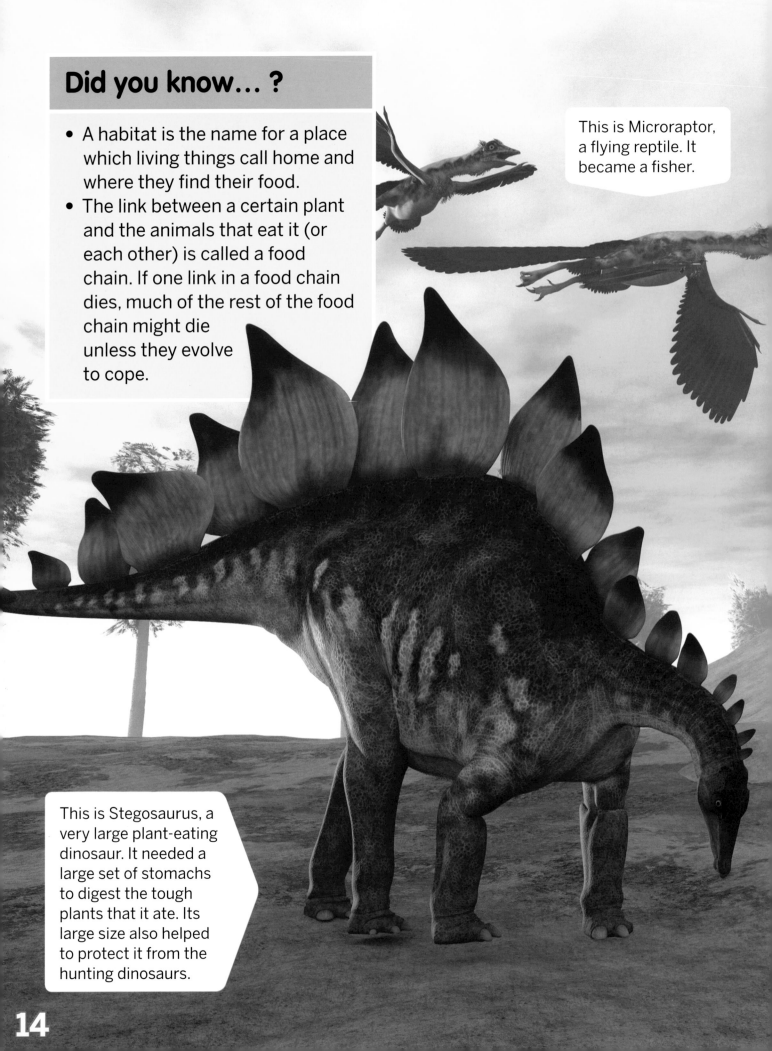

Did you know… ?

- A habitat is the name for a place which living things call home and where they find their food.
- The link between a certain plant and the animals that eat it (or each other) is called a food chain. If one link in a food chain dies, much of the rest of the food chain might die unless they evolve to cope.

This is Microraptor, a flying reptile. It became a fisher.

This is Stegosaurus, a very large plant-eating dinosaur. It needed a large set of stomachs to digest the tough plants that it ate. Its large size also helped to protect it from the hunting dinosaurs.

Habitats

The world has lots of different kinds of living things. The most important of all are the plants. They use sunlight, water and soil to grow. Animals cannot do this – they must eat plants, or one another.

For plants to be successful, they must be able to grow in wet places, in dry places and so on. Plants survive in each environment by adapting. In a desert, for example, they adapt by evolving to have small leaves, deep roots and stems that hold water.

If animals adapt, too, then many kinds of animal can live together, each eating a different kind of plant. This makes the best use of the food available.

This is Allosaurus, a hunting dinosaur something like T-rex, but a bit smaller. (It is a different **species**.) In order to hunt other dinosaurs it had to move fast, so large hind legs and big tooth-filled jaws would have been an advantage.

Q Why did the hunting dinosaurs evolve large back legs?

Catastrophes

Our planet goes around the Sun more or less regularly. But there are lumps of rock out in space that do not follow regular paths. Some of the most dangerous are called asteroids. They are very large pieces of rock moving at tremendous speeds. Just occasionally over the life of the Earth asteroids have hit the planet, and when that happened they caused huge changes to the weather, and many living things that could not adapt died out.

For example, about 65 million years ago an asteroid collision changed the world of the dinosaurs, and many other animals. They almost all died out.

But this left opportunities for other animals. For example, **mammals** were given the chance to thrive in a world where they no longer had to compete with reptiles.

Nobody really knows what happened 65 million years ago, but it was quite sudden and dinosaurs did not survive it. The impact could have put so much dust in the air that it made the Earth colder. As reptiles need warm conditions, they could not survive the cold period that followed.

Did you know… ?

- Huge events like asteroids hitting the Earth only happen once every two hundred million years or more.
- The plants and animals that survive have the whole world to live in, so they can change to fit into all environments, and so become more varied.
- Change will affect animals and plants on land more than in the oceans because the ocean waters keep a steadier environment.
- Some dinosaur-like reptiles did survive – for example the crocodile.

 What happened 65 million years ago?

A new beginning

With reptiles out of the way, the last 65 million years has been the time of the mammals. We are mammals – creatures that give birth to live young, and nurse them by giving them milk.

But people only evolved towards the end of this period, perhaps the last five million years, although our relatives – primates – developed about 55 million years ago.

Being warm-blooded, they could live in more places than reptiles.

This is one of the mammals that developed after the age of dinosaurs. It is a hornless rhinoceros and is the largest land mammal ever to have lived. It was 5m tall at the shoulder and weighed 11 tonnes. It lived about 30 million years ago.

Q What are mammals?

Did you know... ?

- Mammals are warm-blooded animals.
- Primates – except for humans, apes and baboons – tend to live in the trees of tropical forests.
- Primates include lemurs and monkeys.
- Ninety-eight percent of our DNA is the same as chimpanzees.
- Primates have large brains compared to other mammals.
- Primates make more use of their sight, and less use of their sense of smell, than other mammals.

Moving continents

The land we live on seems literally rock solid. You can't imagine it moving, can you? But it does. The Earth's surface crust is split into great slabs like a 3-D jigsaw. Many of these slabs are about the same as the **continents**. And they move. They move at about the same rate as your fingernails grow. But over millions of years that adds up.

Continents have always been on the move. But because they fit together, if they are to move, they must crush into one another (which is what makes mountains) in the direction they are moving, and on the far sides they must pull away (leaving oceans like the Atlantic Ocean).

Because continents move apart like this, animals and plants on one continent can easily get separated from those on another continent. And then they evolve separately. This is why plants and animals in America are different from those in Europe. The same is true of Australia and New Zealand.

Did you know… ?

- If you lived for 100 million years, your fingernails would be 5,000km long – which is how far America has moved away from Europe in the same time.
- Continents move from one part of the Earth to another. This often takes them from the tropics to the poles. That is what happened to Antarctica. Most living things could not evolve fast enough to cope with cold conditions, so they died out.

America

Bald eagle (America)

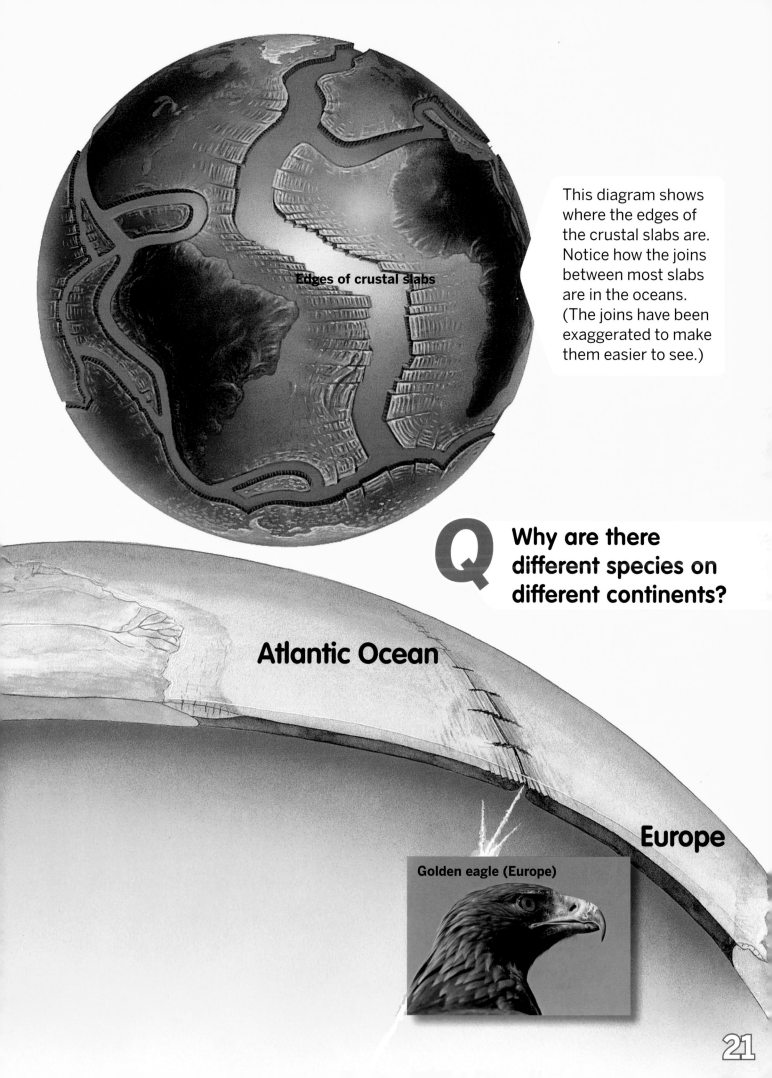

Edges of crustal slabs

This diagram shows where the edges of the crustal slabs are. Notice how the joins between most slabs are in the oceans. (The joins have been exaggerated to make them easier to see.)

Q Why are there different species on different continents?

Atlantic Ocean

Europe

Golden eagle (Europe)

Ice Age

An Ice Age is an example of a time when things change fairly quickly, but not catastrophically.

In an Ice Age the whole Earth cools down a little, so the ice sheets spread out from the poles and cover up to about a third of the world. The last Ice Age began about two million years ago.

The area near the Equator stays warm, so living things can live there without change. The other thing they can do is to evolve ways of coping with the cold. They can get bigger and hairier. Woolly mammoths, rhinoceroses and polar bears did this. But if the Ice Age ends quickly, they may find they have no cold places left to live, and they will die out. Woolly mammoths and rhinoceroses are already **extinct**; the polar bear may follow.

Did you know… ?

- Big bodies lose less heat than small ones because they have a smaller surface area compared to their bulk.
- Stone Age people were around even before the Ice Age.
- People did not evolve quickly, but they coped with the Ice Age by wearing clothes, living in caves and learning about fire.

Woolly mammoth

Woolly rhinoceros

Q **What is the difference between the way a mammoth coped with the Ice Age, and people?**

Can we see things evolve?

Evolution is often very slow. But some evolution is very fast. So there are two ways we can find out about evolution: by looking back at fossils to see how they have changed, and by studying those things that are changing fast now.

How quickly something can change depends on how long it lives for, and how quickly it can produce young. The fastest changes tend to occur in small things that **breed** quickly. It means they can adapt quickly.

Bacteria

The best case of rapid evolution is bacteria. Bacteria are microbes, far too small to see except with powerful microscopes. They can reproduce every fifteen minutes or so. There are also trillions upon trillions of them. So when we try to kill them off by using medicines called antibiotics, there is a good chance that not all get killed.

It only takes a few to have the special properties that keep them safe, and allow them to continue to breed.

Soon we have to find a new medicine to kill the survivors.

The problem never goes away because some will always evolve and not be affected by whatever we do. If bacteria lived a hundred years, and only bred once a year, then we would have a better chance of killing them off.

You can see why doctors are so worried about giving antibiotics. The more often the antibiotics are given, the more chances some bacteria have of learning how to adapt. So the faster they change, the sooner the antibiotic will no longer work. That is why doctors have been told to hold back on antibiotics unless really necessary. It is the evolution battle in action.

The Galapagos finches

The famous Galapagos Islands in the Pacific Ocean are completely isolated by being in the middle of a large ocean, so the living things must adapt (evolve) where they are or die out.

The Medium Ground Finch is a species of bird which lives only on the Galapagos Islands. The place where it lives is dry forests. The species was the first where scientists have observed large animals changing (evolving) in a short period of time.

In 1977, a severe drought meant there were fewer seeds on the forest trees. The finch, which eats small and soft seeds, was forced to turn to harder, larger seeds. As you might imagine, those birds with slightly bigger beaks were able to eat these seeds more easily, and so they did not starve. As a result, over the last forty years, these finches have changed so that they have, on average, beaks that are a tenth bigger than they used to be.

Q Why is evolution a problem for doctors?

Variation

Do you have brothers and sisters, or cousins? Are they identical to you? Probably not. You will have some features in common, but you will have a lot of differences. That is because nature almost never produces identical offspring – children, puppies or anything else.

Why not? It is all about being able to survive. The more slight variations there are, the more it is likely that the same catastrophe won't affect them all. If things are all exactly the same, they stand a risk of being wiped out by a single disease or a change in climate. And we see this doesn't happen. Instead, variation helps living things to evolve to meet the needs of changing environments.

Did you know…?

- In the past, when people could not treat an infection like the Plague (also called the Black Death), up to forty percent of all people died. But the others didn't because they were resistant to it. This was because they were slightly different to those that died. As a result, the Plague could not harm them.

Q How many differences can you spot between these five 'pure-bred' boxer puppies?

Are giraffes weird?

Giraffes look so strange, with their long necks and purple tongues. But are they really weird, or just very successful at what they do?

Animals all live together in any place, and if a species can adapt to reach food in a way no other species can, it will be successful and survive. They can adapt this way if they are naturally varied. For example, the chances of some developing long necks or long legs will be good. Because they will be able to reach food others can't, they are more likely to survive in a drought. They will have long-necked offspring, so long-necked animals will become more common.

The giraffe is a good example. It browses for tree leaves. It can reach far higher than any other animal except an elephant. So in times of drought, a giraffe can often find food when others can't. Giraffes have to splay out their legs to drink, but in comparison to dying of hunger in a drought, this is a tiny problem.

Drinking

Browsing

Eating

Q Do you think giraffes are very varied?

Did you know... ?

- Giraffes are 6m tall and weigh one and a half tonnes.
- They can live in grasslands, shrublands and woodlands.
- Giraffes can wrap their tongues around thorny branches and take leaves without being hurt by the thorns.
- Giraffes sleep standing up by locking the joints in their legs.
- Giraffes evolved near Turkey about 8 million years ago and migrated to Africa, which is now their main home.
- The Asian giraffes died out in the Ice Age, but the African ones – in warmer climates – thrived.

Siblings

People

People are like all living things and they live by the same rules: the rules of evolution.

You have already learned that we are descended from a line of animals that began fifty five million years ago (the primates), and that most of those ancestors lived in tropical forests.

The earliest ancestors that look enough like us to be called people lived several million years ago. Their remains have only been found in Africa, which suggests that all of us are descended from tropical Africans.

When we learned how to use tools to do more than any other animal, we became very different from any other living thing. This time was called the Stone Age.

People seem to have spread out from Africa to other parts of the world, and as they did so, many of them changed and developed slightly separately. That is why people have different skin colours, for example.

There is no reason to suppose people are not still evolving. I wonder what we will be like in another four million years?

The skull of Neanderthal man.

The first tool-using man
(2 million years ago)

Upright man
(1 million years ago)

Upright man
(200,000 years ago)

There were at least two different kinds of people in the early Stone Age world. One kind had a big forehead. They were called Neanderthals. The others were like us. Gradually the Neanderthals died out, while our direct ancestors continued to evolve. We know all this by finding ancient skulls.

Q **How are people changing now?**

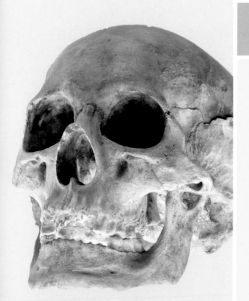

The skull of modern man.

Did you know… ?

- DNA tests suggest that people became a separate species from chimpanzees about six to seven million years ago.
- As people have evolved, so their brain size has got bigger.
- Our species developed separately from the Neanderthals about 500,000 years ago. We are called Homo sapiens (wise man).
- People change fastest when they move to areas with different environments, such as cold or drought.

Glossary

atmosphere
The air around the Earth.

breed
To make new living things.

cell
The smallest building block of living things. A cell contains DNA which it can use to produce new offspring.

continent
A very large area of land separate or nearly separate from other large areas of land.

extinct species
A species that once lived on Earth, but does so no longer.

insulator
A material that does not let heat through easily.

mammal
An animal that gives birth to live young and feeds them milk.

microbe
A very small living thing (bacteria, for example).

molten
A word to describe a hot liquid that has just formed from a solid.

species
A group of living things that can breed with one another.

Index

Curriculum Visions

Curriculum Visions Explorers
This series provides straightforward introductions to key worlds and ideas.

You might also be interested in
Our other books such as Exploring the world of fossils, Exploring the first civilisations, The Stone Age, Celtic times, The ancient Egyptians, The ancient Greeks, The Romans in Britain and Ancient Rome.

www.CurriculumVisions.com

(Subscription required)

© Atlantic Europe Publishing 2014

The right of Brian Knapp to be identified as the author of this work has been asserted by him in accordance with the Copyright, Designs and Patents Act 1988.

Author
Brian Knapp, BSc, PhD

Senior Designer
Adele Humphries, BA, PGCE

Editors
Gillian Gatehouse
Emily Pulsford, BA

Illustrations
Mark Stacey 22-23
David Woodroffe 10, 12, 21

Designed and produced by
Atlantic Europe Publishing

Printed in China by
WKT Company Ltd

**Exploring evolution
– Curriculum Visions
A CIP record for this book is available from the British Library.**

Paperback ISBN 978 1 78278 073 1

Picture credits
All photographs and illustrations are from the Earthscape and ShutterStock Picture Libraries unless separately credited above.

This product is manufactured from sustainable managed forests. For every tree cut down at least one more is planted.